GOD'S LOVE

My Life as a Service Dog

by

Gottlieb

as told to

Thomas Martin

Wasteland Press
Shelbyville, KY USA
www.wastelandpress.net

God's Love:
My Life as a Service Dog
by Thomas Martin

First Printing – March 2022
Paperback ISBN: 978-1-68111-458-3
Hardback ISBN: 978-1-68111-462-0
Library of Congress Control Number: 2022904742

Cover Design by Brian Hirakami
Cover Photograph by Kimi Yokota
www.TMartinBooks.com

Printed in the U.S.A.

0 1 2 3 4

For Steve and Gottlieb

&

To all those who help people in need

ACKNOWLEDGEMENTS

We would like to thank the following people for their help, inspiration, and contributions to this very special project:

Steven Blackman

Butch Blackman

Terri Blackman

Sandy Moore

Kimi Yokota

Erin LaMonte

Mikell Bollinger

Bill Hooten

David Norcott

Judge Ed Kinkeade

Mel Gottlieb

Sara Franke

Barbara Peznowski

Barbara Katzka

Canine Companions®

TABLE OF CONTENTS

INTRODUCTION

"For I know the plans I have for you," declares the Lord, "plans to prosper you and not to harm you, plans to give you hope and a future."

– Jeremiah 29:11

It is always overwhelming to see God's plan unfold in our lives. Around 2008, I met a woman in a dog park in Southern California along with her puppy who was wearing a yellow and blue service vest. She told me she was a volunteer puppy raiser for Canine Companions for Independence® now called simply Canine Companions®. This brief encounter laid the groundwork for what has culminated in this book.

In May 2012 I moved to the Dallas/Fort Worth area of Texas. Soon thereafter, I became a member of the Lions Club, an international service organization. Through that club I became more closely associated with Canine Companions, eventually becoming a fundraiser for Lions Project for Canine Companions (a Lions entity that supports only Canine Companions with the donations of various individual Lions Clubs).

About this time, Canine Companions opened their newest regional facility in Irving, Texas, just east of Fort Worth. Because of my own club's donation, we were invited to the first open house. During that event I met Steve and heard how his service dog, Gottlieb, changed his life. The story stuck with me and I periodically drew from it when I spoke to Lions Clubs about this amazing organization that breeds, raises, and trains service dogs for almost any challenge or disability other than vision. They also provide these incredible animals at no cost to their clients.

I continued running into Steve at various Canine Companions events and then lost touch with him.

Surprisingly, he re-appeared in my life as a candidate joining the same Masonic lodge at which I attend. We re-established our relationship and Steve joined me for a presentation I was doing promoting Canine Companions.

This started a discussion about my writing his biography which eventually morphed into this little book. In the time I have known Steve, I have been amazed as to the extent his service dog, Gottlieb, changed his life. I felt compelled to put the story down in print, both to honor Gottlieb, honor Steve, and make more people aware of Canine Companions.

This book is part fantasy but mostly factual. Obviously, I cannot get into Gottlieb's head and read his thoughts, but through my interviews with Gottlieb's puppy raiser, his trainers, and Steve – I don't think I am too far off track.

Please note that throughout the story, I am primarily relaying Gottlieb's thoughts, therefore his thoughts are not contained within quote marks. Conversely, the words of the various humans in the story are within quotes to distinguish them.

I am very blessed to be a part of this organization, to know Steve, and to be able to write this story. I hope you enjoy it and find it as touching as I did as I wrote it. Writing this story was a very emotional experience for me. I had to get into the heart and soul of both Steve and Gottlieb and I shed a lot of tears doing so, because it touched me that deeply.

Enjoy!

Chapter 1: I Am Born

Wow! I don't know what just happened, but I am certainly not too happy about it. Everything was warm, cozy, quiet, and dark and now everything is bright, cold, and loud. I can see, but just barely, it's simply too bright here and so I keep my eyes mostly closed.

There is something else new; I feel a pang in my stomach. I don't know what it is, but I know I need to do something about it and *soon*. Before I have a chance to look around, a wide, wet object runs itself all over my body, over and over again. I look up and can just barely see this enormous creature above me. Apparently, she is my mother and she is bathing me. She is so beautiful, so kind, and so loving that it almost makes what just happened seem okay.

I finally notice that the others with whom I shared the previous space are near me and are crawling toward our mother. I join the flow and discover the most extraordinary thing, a small, soft, pink object on our mother's belly. I see the others attaching themselves to one, so I do the same.

You won't even believe what happened next! This white, warm liquid flowed out and into my mouth. It was all so new and wonderful, and as I kept doing this, that nasty new pang in my stomach started going away!

Well, maybe things aren't as bad as I first thought.

Just when I am getting used to my first meal, I find myself floating in the air. Something is pinching the back of my neck and I rise higher and higher in the air. I am just starting to be a little concerned when I begin moving sideways. I stop and am lying on the chest of a creature far larger than my mother. She is so warm and loving, though. I sniff around for one of those pink things, as I would like more of that warm liquid, but, alas, there are none. On the other hand, she cuddles me and talks to me. I can feel the vibration in her chest as she tells me, "You sweet little puppy, you are going to change someone's life one day. To that person, you will be a gift from God."

I don't know how I know what she is saying, but I do. I think "*ME*? I'm going to change someone's life? Are you serious? I can barely see!" I decide to ask her, but when I open my mouth, all I can make are funny squeaky noises, so I quit trying. I do suspect this woman is overly optimistic, but she is sweet and loving and she puts me back with the others, next to my mother. I decide I'll think more about it later. Right now, I'm going enjoy more of this white stuff. Then, I think I'm going to take a nap, I'm feeling a bit sleepy. <yawn>

Chapter 2: I Have a Name!

You should see me now! I have grown so much! I'm a big dog, I can even walk around on my four feet, I'm not merely crawling, like I used to. I'm still not as big as my mom, but I am quickly catching up to her.

The nice lady gave us each a present the other day, mine was a red collar. I don't really like wearing it, but the lady told me how handsome I look with my black fur and the red collar, so I decided to just be polite, say thank you, smile and wag my tail.

Today, several nice people came to visit us. We learn that we are part of a program called Canine Companions in Santa Rosa, California. We will be trained as service dogs in the near future and today they decide to give us names. We are part of what is referred to as the "G" litter. Every member of my litter receives a name starting with "G." A nice man picks me up, looks me in the eye and says, "Your name is Gottlieb. You are a very special boy as you are named after one of our directors, Mel Gottlieb. Mel says that your name means 'God's Love'." Wow, I am being named after a very important man. Hey, maybe that nice lady was right, maybe I truly am something special.

From all the people who have come to see me and the others, there sure is a lot of excitement. Everyone wants to pick us up and cuddle. Not that I mind, I assure you. It's really quite wonderful and everyone keeps telling us what special dogs we are and how we are going to change people's lives. So far, I'm not certain how this is going to happen, but I'll do my best to keep an open mind.

The box where we live is filled with these wonderful, soft, plush toys and we all love to play, chew, and tumble with them. We also play with each other until we are simply too tired to play anymore, then we usually nap. I sure sleep a lot! I don't know how I will be able to help anyone when all I ever want to do is sleep! Our mom leaves us alone now and then. I think we tire her out and she needs a break. I guess I understand, but her leaving also means "no food" until she returns.

I'm still surprised at the number of things I already know and understand. I can actually feel the emotions coming off the people who visit us and I always understand what it is they are saying when they talk.

I hear them talk about the volunteer puppy raisers, the people who are going to raise us. I'm not sure when these people are coming over, but I think my mom would like to check them out first, I know I would!

Chapter 3: The Dream

<gasp> There he is, *THERE HE IS!!* I see him just ahead of me. I know I need him and he needs me. I run and run with all my heart and strength, but I never seem to get closer to him. He's *right* there in front of me, why can't I get to him?

I finally stop running and try barking. Maybe if he sees me, he'll come to me. I bark and bark, but he never looks down. I can see you; can't you see me? I'm right in front of you!!

He is the red-haired man I keep dreaming about. He is in so much pain and he is so sad. I must get to him to help him, to love him. I need him to know he is not alone.

"Gottlieb! What's going on boy? You were having a dream. Your little legs were running a hundred miles an hour and you were barking. Are you okay?"

I open my eyes and look up. It is the nice lady. She cuddles me and smiles.

I look as deeply into her eyes as I possibly can. I want my heart to connect with her heart. Sweet Lady, do you know the red-haired man? Can you please help me find him?

I look around the room, looking for him. We make a perfect pair. Lady, *please*. Please take me to the red-haired man.

Chapter 4: A New Home

Lately, we have been seeing less and less of our mom. On the other hand (paw?), we are being given many wonderfully tasting foods and have been using our teeth.

Let's talk a bit about teeth. I can't believe these amazing little things. At first, they hurt like the dickens as they were coming in. All I wanted to do all day long is chew on one thing or another. If I could just bite on something hard enough, maybe my teeth would come in and it wouldn't hurt so bad any longer. A couple of times, I even tried biting on the nice lady, something I never thought I would do. She gently tapped my nose, firmly said "don't" and set me back on the floor.

For the most part, my days are spent tussling with the others and playing with the toys the nice lady provides for us.

Well, that was until this morning. Something is different today, very different.

First thing this morning, the nice lady comes and picks each one of us up separately; she cuddles us, and tells us each how much she loves us. As she gives each of us a kiss, she again tells us how special we are. I don't understand why she is so sad.

A little later that morning, several of the people we have seen in the past come in with these small plastic boxes with little fence-like gates on the front. One by one, we are picked up and placed in our own little crate. At first it is fun, but then I decide I don't really like it all that much so I start whining. It doesn't do any good; the people just keep working, putting all of us in the small crates. Repeatedly, I hear the words "airport" and "flights," two words that mean nothing to me.

When they finish, they take us by car to the most incredible place. It is enormous and filled with harsh smells and noises. I don't think I like it here and I really want to go back to the nice lady's house. Before I can protest, my crate and I are being loaded onto this huge tube-like vehicle, much larger than a car, in an area filled with suitcases and crates containing many of the others.

I have to admit, I am a little frightened. I try making myself really small in the corner of the crate. Maybe if I nap, I'll wake up and this will all be a bad dream.

We start moving and then we are moving really, really fast. I think, "if this thing goes any faster, it's going to come up off the ground!" Well, sure enough, that's exactly what happens! We are suddenly up in the air. I wish I wasn't alone in this crate. I wish I had one of the others with me, but I comfort myself with the thought that maybe I'm finally on my way to see the red-haired man!

All of a sudden there is a big bump and I feel this vehicle rapidly slowing down. I have trouble keeping my footing in the crate and I slide back and forth.

When we finally stop, the big door is opened and I see light and people again. There seems to be a lot of interest in me and I am the first one taken out. My crate and I are handed off to an official looking person who takes me around to the side of a big building. Standing there are several people. Everyone is smiling and happy. They all look so nice and they all seem so happy to see me! I look around and still do not see the red-haired man. I'm a little sad, but these people open the small gate to my crate, take me out and start loving and cuddling me. They keep telling me how cute I am! *WELL!* I like to think of myself as handsome, not cute. I'll have to have a talk with them if I decide to stay.

They put me back into my crate and take me to their car. I settle into the back seat with this woman who keeps smiling at me and touching me through the door of the crate. She just keeps giggling and laughing. I'm glad I can make her so happy, even though I'm not really doing anything.

We arrive at this large facility in a city I hear is called Oceanside. This is the regional center for Canine Companions. I notice the crate of one of the others is also in the back seat with me. They take us out of the car and into one of the buildings.

Before I can protest or make a request, I am out of the crate and into a large open tub with water being sprayed on me. Shortly I am covered in soft, bubbly suds and this new lady is massaging me all over. I kind of like the sensation and the water feels wonderful.

When they finish, I am dried off in fluffy towels and set down to air dry for a while. I feel like taking a nap, but before I can act on my decision, I am picked up and taken into another room.

There waiting for me is a lovely family with one young woman with the softest, sweetest voice. She is smiling at me from ear to ear. I'm still amazed at how happy I seem to make people even when I haven't done anything.

As they hand me to this sweet woman she smiles and says, “Wow! He is quite the big boy!”

The woman who holds me replies, “Yep, he is sixteen pounds, one of the biggest pups in this litter”!

The woman talks further with the people from the center, and then we all get into their car and head off. I'm excited but also a bit afraid. I've come so far and yet I have still not found the red-haired man. Is he here in Oceanside? Does he live with these people? He's my reason for being here but I can't seem to explain this to anyone. I hope someone realizes this and makes it all happen!

We arrive at their house and I am taken inside. I'm finally taken out of the crate and get to stand on the floor again <whew>. In addition to the people here, there is another young dog. His name is Bowen and he comes over to greet me. He has the most interesting smell about him, something very familiar to me. We just keep sniffing each other, checking each other out and it seems that he knows there is something familiar about me as well.

Guess what? He is my half-brother! We have the same father. Bowen and I become instant best friends. I like the others who were with me along with my mother, but Bowen is special. We immediately start running around and playing. I am so happy here, but..... I think you've already guessed who is NOT here. So, I am both happy and sad.

Chapter 5: Life in Oceanside

I decide I really like it here. I do miss my mom and the nice lady, but I am having a lot of fun running and playing with Bowen. Together we get to run around outside on this wonderful carpet of grass. The weather is perfect, not too hot and not too cold.

Oh, did I tell you how big I am getting? I'm almost a full-sized dog now. The bad part is that I don't get picked up and cuddled as much as before, but I am treated with more respect. Almost no one calls me "cute" anymore, and I appreciate that. Now I'm almost always called "handsome."

Kimi spends time with me teaching me my name. Repeatedly she calls "Gottlieb" to me. Yes, yes – I know my name, Kimi. I know she wants me to look at her each time she says my name, so I hide my frustrations and simply comply. She is working hard to make me the best service dog possible and I want both of us to look good. I just wish it was easier for me to tell her I pick these tasks and commands up quickly and that I truly understand her. I guess the only way I can communicate that to her is by responding to the commands she gives me as quickly and cooperatively as possible. I smile as I think that soon, she will learn as well.

Kimi introduces me to something I definitely do not like. While we are in the backyard, she places this thing around my nose and has me walk next to her. She tells me she is teaching me how to properly walk. “How silly” I think, “I already know how to walk, and I am actually quite good at it.” Every time I try to run forward, the strap around my nose causes my head to turn back and look at Kimi. When that happens, I can no longer see where I am going, so I just relax, wait for Kimi to catch up and we walk side-by-side again. She is very patient with me and she is always hugging me, talking to me, and giving me kisses and treats. After the first time with the nose lead, I understand I need to only walk beside her on her left side. I don’t think we really need to use the nose lead every single time, but it is just part of the routine, so I do my best to cooperate.

Kimi also introduces me to an interesting toy she calls a Frisbee. In the backyard, she tosses this little disc and it flies gently through the air, landing softly onto the grass. Before she tosses it, she shows it to me, trying to generate interest on my part. Well, it is a lovely shade of blue and all, but it is just a round piece of plastic, after all. How excited can I really get about this thing? I've tried teaching her repeatedly that I am very food motivated. This round piece of plastic really doesn't rise to that status.

She tells me that I am to chase this flying disc across the yard and return it to her. I'm not really certain of the purpose of this, but having a cooperative personality and outlook, I do my best to comply.

As the disc drifts through the air, I saunter along, looking up and following its flight path. Kimi keeps telling me to jump up and catch it. I don't understand why she says this; I already know the disc will soon come down to the ground on its own.

After a while, this game begins to annoy me and I view the disc as being at fault. As it reaches the ground, instead of picking it up, I stalk it and pounce on it. I pick it up with my mouth and shake it a bit, hoping to disable its ability to fly in the future.

I'm not successful and yet again, the disc is soaring over my head. Hmm... Maybe the next attack will stop it?

At least Kimi is laughing along with me rather than being unhappy. I like it when Kimi laughs, she is so sweet and kind to me and I like that I can make her happy and proud, at times.

Kimi also likes dressing me up for holidays. I don't mind too much; I see myself as naturally handsome and that costumes are not really necessary. But it makes her happy and she takes many pictures of me in different poses. She is so nice, so I suppose it is the least I can do for her.

Kimi spends a lot of time working with me. We are making great progress and I know she is very proud of me. I like making her happy and showing her what an excellent service dog I will become. If only I could actually talk to her, it would make things so much easier.

One of my favorite things is when we meet up with other volunteer puppy raisers and their puppies for field trips. We go to the grocery store, the park, the mall. Every place we go has new smells, new sounds and many different people. Bowen and I always do well in these gatherings. We just don't let new things bother us. Some of the other dogs are overly cautious and concerned, but Bowen and I just move forward and blaze a trail for the others.

One day things at home are especially energized. I know something big is up. Kimi comes and looks me over, ensuring I am perfectly groomed. She tells me that I am going to meet a very special person today. All I can think about is the red-haired man and that I will finally help him feel better.

We get into the car and begin driving north. Kimi tells me that we will be meeting the man after whom I am named. He is a donor and director of Canine Companions. His name is Mel Gottlieb and he has come all the way from Australia to meet me! Yes, I need to be on my very best behavior today, I would like to impress this man who was kind enough to share his name with me.

We drive north along the coast for a very long time. When we finally exit the 405 freeway, we are in a city called Beverly Hills. We drive up to a beautiful building and a man opens the car door for me and Kimi. We step out and the man drives the car away. I look at it for a while, wondering how we will get home again, but Kimi seems excited and happy to be at this place, so I follow her in to the building. We are at the Peninsula Hotel on Santa Monica Boulevard. It is a magnificently beautiful place. As we enter the lobby, a very distinguished gentleman walks over to greet us. He has a huge smile on his face and begins speaking to Kimi. Kimi gives me the “release” command, which informs me I am no longer working, I can now relax and be social. Mr. Gottlieb reaches down and gives me some loving touches. I am so honored and impressed to be named after such a fine gentleman. I hope I can live up to my name.

Together we all walk to the dining room of the hotel to have lunch. The place is far more elegant than any place I have visited before and I do my best to stand as tall and proud as I can. Everyone is looking at me and smiling. It is a wonderful, magical place. Mr. Gottlieb has some gifts for me and even pours Evian water from France into a bowl for me to drink. If Kimi isn’t careful, I could easily get used to this kind of treatment!

As everyone eats, the conversation keeps coming back to me. I’m a bit embarrassed but also flattered. Kimi tells Mr. Gottlieb “He is one of the best dogs I have raised, he is very hard working and takes the tasks very seriously. He learns the commands quickly and is always anxious to please me.”

Well, of course, I think. I know why I am here and who I am.

I want nothing more than to ask this gentleman about the red-haired man, but I have the same issues communicating with him as I do with everyone else.

He seems very happy and proud of me and he keeps complimenting Kimi on what a good job she is doing raising me. I am proud; proud that I can make Kimi look so good, she definitely deserves to be praised.

Chapter 6: Matriculation

Matriculation: *The act of enrolling at a college or university*

Something is different lately. Kimi seems sad and a bit distant. I try doing things to make her smile, but she doesn't laugh as easily as before. I hope she is alright.

It doesn't take long before I understand what is happening. One day, Kimi gets me all brushed and looking especially handsome and we head out to the car. After a fairly short drive, we turn into a complex of buildings that look vaguely familiar. I know I have been here before, but I can't quite remember when.

We both get out of the car and I see many people walking around and many other dogs about my size. Most of the people seem happy but there are many others, like Kimi, who seem sad. While walking through the crowd, I keep my eyes out for the red-haired man, but I don't see him here either. Now I am a bit sad as well.

Kimi takes me inside one of the buildings and then it dawns on me.... This is where they first brought me after leaving my mother! This is where I first met Kimi! While I am looking and sniffing around, someone places a yellow and blue cape on me. I see other dogs with this same cape and many more without them. Clearly, we are special, but I don't know why.

Kimi takes me over to an area where a man is taking pictures of those of us wearing the capes along with our puppy raisers. Again, everyone seems a bit sad and that makes me sad too.

After some sort of "graduation" ceremony, where I see other dogs being handed off to people, Kimi leads me to one of the workers here at the Canine Companions regional facility. Kimi hands my leash to this lovely woman who reaches down, gives me a loving pat, and leads me down a hallway. I know in my heart that there is more training ahead. Maybe this is just the next step before I can finally meet the red-haired man.

I proudly walk down the hall and then fully realize that Kimi won't be here with me. I'm both excited and very sad now.

I am taken to a new kennel and placed inside. It is similar to the one Kimi keeps at home for me, but the place is not as warm and cozy. There are many like me being placed in these kennels. We are all looking around and wondering what exactly is happening and what awaits us at this new home.

Chapter 7: The Accident – May 2008

"Steve? Steve? Can you hear me? Please open your eyes."

"Yea, what? What's going on? Where am I?"

"Steve, you have been in an accident and are in the hospital at Fort Carson in Colorado. We are caring for you."

"Accident? Are you joking? What kind of accident?"

"It was a training accident. You fell off the back of a truck. We initially thought you broke your back. Instead, we found that you sustained injuries to your head. At first, it seemed to be only a mild concussion, but now we know that the back lobes of your brain had a small separation and bruising. Physically, you seem to be in pretty good shape, but we still need to determine how this might affect you mentally. Steve, can you tell me what time it is?"

I know to look at the face of the clock, but the characters around the perimeter mean nothing to me. Something is very wrong with me, but I don't want to admit it to myself or to the nurse.

"No, I cannot. I know that the clock should give me that information, but I do not understand the characters on the face. I'm sorry, I cannot help you."

"Not to worry, it is probably just some of the side effects of the drugs we have been giving you. Give it time and it should resolve itself."

But it does not resolve itself. I see fellow soldiers, I know that I know them, but am unable to think of their names. I have to resort to looking at the name tapes on their uniforms.

I try my best to remember things, but it is as if pockets of information have been erased.

In my room, I finally have to label the objects and keep my driver's license and military ID next to my bed. In this way, I can wake up, check my identification, be reminded of my name and know that I am in the US Army.

As I explore the room, Post-it notes remind me what is a table, a chair, a desk, a lamp, a book, and so forth. My short-term and long-term memories have both been compromised and progress is slow. I have also lost all math ability and comprehension.

Chapter 8: Advanced Training

Well, I *thought* I was to start further training, instead it seems that I have landed in some sort of hospital. Every day there are tests and more tests. Everything is examined and considered. Apparently Canine Companions wants nothing but the very best dogs. This includes physically, mentally, and I assume, behaviorally.

So far, there is nothing too difficult, I'm just ready to get to work and they just want to keep looking me over.

Well, pretty soon they will realize that I am one of the best and they need to let me move on to fulfill my destiny. After all, *I am Gottlieb!*

That day comes and instead of being paraded into the medical areas, I am taken into a room and a lovely woman begins teaching me new commands. Much like Kimi, I need to teach this woman that I learn quickly and being overly repetitive is just annoying to me. I'm here to learn, but I'm also ready to work. I am confident enough that I believe I can skip much of this training. I'll have to ask if I can merely audit or test-out of many of these classes.

I have settled into the routine here, almost every day there is some reviewing of previous training, some new training, and some time spent simply being quiet and still. Oh, and they also let us go outside and run and play together. That is my favorite part by far!

I always seem to receive extra attention and praise from the staff. I am often taken off the facility grounds and used in presentations, they say it is because I behave so well and perform the commands so perfectly. I'd blush, but my face is covered with black fur, so, who would know?

Chapter 9: The Long Road Home - 2010

"I just want to stay in the military. Isn't there *something* I can do? I'm even willing to merely teach privates how to throw hand grenades in basic training. The military is my life, it is all I've ever wanted. Please don't send me home."

"Steve, you know things don't work that way in the Army. We want to get you all the help we can, but your remaining on active duty is simply not possible."

It was as if that hand grenade exploded in my gut. I know he is right, but it is almost impossible for me to accept. In addition to the chronic physical pain I am experiencing, now I must face the depressing realization that my life's plans and hopes have ended. For two years I have fought to find a place within the military for someone like me and with no success. I watched all of the friends I made in Colorado get their orders to go, leaving me behind. I am lonely, depressed, and in serious pain.

I also have serious mobility issues and depending on the day, I may have to use a power chair, a walker, or a cane.

The pain I experience is so severe that I am taking the maximum dose of pain medications three times a day. It is at a level that would never be prescribed for civilians. Being at this high level for two years is taking its toll on me. First of all, I have developed an immunity to the pain meds. In spite of taking them three times a day, I am still in extreme pain. I am also experiencing all of the negative long-term side effects of being on these pills. I realize that something has to change and I tell my doctors I want to go off all medications. I decide that a natural immunity or tolerance to the chronic pain is a better option. The doctors question my decision and caution me, but I move forward and stop cold turkey. Not even realizing I was fully addicted, I go through all of the classic withdrawal symptoms. I suffer terribly over the next two weeks but I survive.

At the end of the two weeks, my body has purged itself of all of the toxins and what is left is the chronic pain in my back and extremities that I expected. I decide I prefer living this way rather than on all of the pills.

It is finally time to go back home to Texas.

Seeing my parents is more painful than the entire prior experience. The pained look on my mother's face when she sees me is almost more than I can bear. Up to now, it has just been me dealing with me, I was the only one in pain. Now that circle is larger and I feel I am hurting those I love most.

Over time, I meet a woman and we begin dating, she fully realizing all of my limitations and issues. We begin building a life together and eventually marry. She works during the day and I am at home. I try to keep myself busy with video games and television but realize I have a strong need to be useful and to contribute. Using my military background, I figure the least I can do is keep the apartment clean and neat. The problem is that I tend to drop things and then am unable to pick them up. The more I work to make things better the worse they become. When my wife comes home from a long day of work, she then has to work to fix all of the problems I created while trying to "help out."

In trying to deal with my depression by being useful and helpful, I seem to be making things worse. I am reaching the end of my rope. There doesn't seem to be a place for me any longer in this world. What can a man like me do if I can't even perform the most basic tasks in life? What good am I to anyone?

I think back to my co-worker in Colorado who had a service dog named Harper. I remember how Harper helped him both physically and emotionally and I begin wondering if I can get one as well. I go online and search for organizations that provide these dogs in Texas. In each case I run into the same obstacles, mostly the cost. "Yes, we can train a dog for you, but it costs about $50,000." Well, that isn't going to happen, I know that.

In spite of these obstacles, something inside of me knows there is a dog out there just waiting for me. I begin talking to everyone I can about my idea and finally one day at the VA clinic, I meet and tell a man my plight and he suggests an organization I had never come across in my research, Canine Companions (Canine.org).

When I get home, I look up Canine Companions on the internet and discover they are based in California. Well, that explains why I never found them earlier, I was limiting my searches to Texas. I find a regional facility in Oceanside, California and give them a call. The lady who talks to me is so sweet and kind and seems to sincerely want to help me. Unlike all of the other organizations to which I have spoken, Canine Companions provides these dogs at no charge to the client.

Ok, this just might work for me! I immediately fill out the online application and sit back to wait with renewed hope in my heart. It is October 2011 and maybe something amazing can happen going forward. My heart is full, and somehow I *know* this is the answer.

Although clients typically wait one to two years from the time they first apply to being called in for Team Training, the fates are on my side and things move rapidly. Not long after submitting my full application and pictures of our apartment, I receive a call from Canine Companions wanting to do a phone interview. We have a good talk about my life and situation and the call ends with them telling me they will get back to me soon. Again, I almost cannot believe how kind and helpful they all seem to be.

In no time at all, they call again inviting me to come to California for a face-to-face interview. My wife and I pack up the stuff we need and head out. Flying is quite difficult for me, but I am excited and hopeful and am ready to start this next chapter in my life. I push through the pain and the challenges and off to California we go.

The interview goes well and we both continue being impressed with every aspect of Canine Companions, the people, the campus, and the possibilities they offer.

Afterward, we return home to Texas and wait.

Chapter 10: The Call – January 2012

"Steve, are your bags packed? We'd like to invite you to Team Training starting Monday, January thirtieth."

It is only the second week of January when I get that magical call. Later in the month is my birthday and it is the best present I can ever hope to receive.

My wife and I quickly make the arrangements necessary to return to Oceanside, California. We decide to arrive a couple of days early, on the weekend, so that we have time to relax and explore the area along the Southern California coast.

We arrive in Oceanside and explore the small beach city. We take time to drive down to the beach and watch the sunset one evening. I know *that* setting sun represents the end of many of my problems and frustrations, but I cannot even dream of how radically and amazingly they will actually change.

Chapter 11: Team Training

Okay, something is up. Ten of us are being moved into the large activities room in the facility. Our crates are lined up and stacked along one wall. There is excitement in the air as the staff works to prepare everything. For what? I do not yet know.

My training seems to be complete and everyone is very happy and excited for me. Maybe this is finally the moment for which I have been waiting. Maybe now, yes, maybe. I've been saying maybe far too many times, though. Maybe this is just another day with another set of people. I need to rein in what seems to be a mere fantasy and just take the days as they come.

Tables are set up around the room and name cards are placed in front of the various chairs. Even though I understand what people say, I have never mastered reading their words.

It is difficult remaining calm because I just know good things are about to happen.

"I need everyone to come in, look for your name cards and take your seats. You will find a notebook at your place that you will use throughout team training. You can begin familiarizing yourself with the book and we will start shortly."

I almost stop breathing when I see the people entering the large room. There are so many and so many who clearly need help. People in power chairs, some with breathing and feeding tubes, some who seem to be very afraid or confused. There in the back, slowly making his way to his table, is the red-haired man. It is *him*, I know it in my heart and in my soul. He isn't just a fantasy, he *is* real! How do I make him look at me? I am not supposed to bark or behave badly, but I so desperately want him to notice me. Has he been dreaming of me as well? I decide to just keep eye contact on him. At some point, I know he will notice me. I know we are supposed to be together.

I see him and the lady checking us all out. I can barely contain myself!

"Honey, look at all of the dogs! They all look to be Labrador retrievers."

"Steve, I was reading the literature and they are Labradors and golden retrievers and a mix of the two."

"Wow, look at this beast, he is so big, powerful, and sleek. His name is Goliath. This is the dog for me, I think."

No, No, No – don't look at him!! Look at me! I'm Gottlieb, I'm the dog you need, don't you know it already? I do!

"Steve, I don't know. We need to find out what the staff thinks is best for you."

"Look at the people here and their physical limitations. How can I possibly take one of these dogs away from someone who may need it more than I do? Am I being selfish?"

"There are more dogs here than people in the class, I doubt you are depriving anyone of anything. Besides, you are deserving as well. Steve, look at this dog. He hasn't taken his eyes off of you since we entered the room."

"Yeah, I see him. What is his name? G-O-T-T-L-I-E-B? What kind of name is that? How do you even pronounce it? I see that it is a male, but what do the letters LGX mean?"

"It just means that he is a Labrador/golden retriever mix, Steve"

Yes, IT'S ME!! Gottlieb!! I'm here for you. Your name is Steve? <sigh> Finally... I know who you are!

"Honey, I don't know how I'll be able to read through all of this material. You are going to have to help me."

"No problem, Steve, we'll get through it together"

"Wow, this gets into everything, they were established in 1975, it talks about the high standards of their breeding program, their regional facilities, the history of the organization, and look, here are all of the commands we need to learn! Yep, I'll need your help. Look, these dogs are not only trained to help veterans and others with challenges similar to mine, they also serve individuals with physical, cognitive or developmental disabilities. They also train dogs for facilities such as hospitals, classrooms, and courthouses."

Two days go by and Steve still does not pay any attention to me. What do I need to do? How can I let him know that I am his dog and always have been? Steve, I'm ready to work – let's get going!

This morning the staff comes to the crates and lets us all out. We get to run over to the people and greet them. I know Steve will notice me now; I won't let him *NOT* notice me!

"We want each of the students to select a dog, come to the front of the class and give the dog some of the basic commands you have learned."

"Honey, I'm going to take Goliath up there. I'd really like to be paired with him."

"Steve, I think you should take Gottlieb."

"I can't even pronounce his name, how on earth can I possibly give him commands?"

<sigh> He's taking that other dog up to the front. That's a mistake. That dog doesn't understand Steve like I do. I guess I just have to sit back and let him fail before he realizes I am the dog for him.

"Well, that didn't go well, the dog barely even looked at me."

"Steve, I've been trying to tell you, look at Gottlieb again, he never takes his eyes off of you! I think he might be the best dog for you!"

Chapter 12: Teams are Formed – Thursday

"Today we match you with the dog we feel best meets your needs. It may not be the dog you think is best for you, but, trust us, we have been doing this a long time and we rarely make a bad match."

"Steve, don't be too disappointed if you don't get Goliath. You shouldn't even be surprised if you don't. He really didn't seem to interact well with you."

"Yes, I know, but who else then?"

Me, Steve! *ME!* Gottlieb! I'm your boy.

When the staff calls out Steve's name and then tell him he is paired with me, I almost leap out of my crate. YES! YES!! I've *always* known this would happen!

"Oh boy, I've got the dog whose name I can't pronounce. How is this going to work?"

"Now, we want everyone to take their dog and follow us outside to the obstacle course."

Oh boy, oh boy. I finally get the chance to show Steve what I can do. He'll know I'm the one, very soon he'll realize that we need each other.

"An obstacle course, like in basic training? That is something I simply cannot do."

"Steve, it can't possibly be something that difficult."

I'm on my very best behavior as I walk outside with Steve. I feel so very proud. The obstacle course is a series of orange cones and we walk together through the course while the staff observes us. I know this is a critical step in the matching process, so I take a deep breath and vow to work perfectly with Steve. I don't want anyone to take me away from him after all this time.

As we walk, I can feel the pain that Steve is feeling. I want him to sit down and rest. I want to lie beside him and help take away his pain and troubles. But he is tough and determined and he presses on. I stay with him and together we complete the course perfectly.

"That was amazing. That dog is perfect, he knows what I want and need before I can even say anything. I just wish I could pronounce his name. I have this new sense of freedom sweeping over me. I can't even explain it. I was so wrong about the other dog. *This* is *my* dog. Of that I have no doubt. I just need to go back inside and write his name down in the training manual to help me remember."

"Steve, I am so happy for you. Like I said before, Gottlieb has had his eyes only on you from the moment we walked in here. I think it is just supposed to happen this way."

Chapter 13: My New Life Begins – Friday Morning

"Honey, I can't sit here any longer. I am just hurting too much. I need to go back to the room and lie down. Can you just bring me up to speed later?"

"No problem Steve, take it easy. Maybe Gottlieb and I will stop by for a visit during lunch."

He's leaving! Where is he going? Take me with you, I'll help you! I can tell he is in so much pain, but he just pushes through it and keeps walking away.

I'll just lie here quietly and hopefully he will be back soon.

But he doesn't return.

After a while, everyone gets up and starts moving around. The lady takes my leash and says, "Gottlieb, let's go check on Steve. See how he is doing."

YES! YES! Steve!

We walk across the campus to the cabins. I've never been inside these buildings, so I am very curious about what is in here. We enter a room and there lying on the bed is Steve. Seeing him makes me happy but it also breaks my heart. I can see how he is struggling. He looks up and smiles at me. I walk over to the bed and he says,

"Gottlieb, Jump!"

Wait, hold on. I'm not allowed up on furniture. Did he really command me to jump?

"I know boy, I know you are not supposed to jump up on furniture, but I need you up here with me."

That's all I need to hear. Steve needs me just as I need him. I immediately leap up onto the bed, being careful not to hurt him. Once near him I sniff over his body trying to assess what is wrong. I can feel the physical pain he feels throughout my entire body. I can also smell his sorrow and frustrations. I lie down next to him and put my head on his chest. I decide it is not enough and I also place my front feet on his chest as well.

Together we just lie quietly. I decide that I will do my best to heal him.

“Honey, you aren’t going to believe this, but it is as if there is a sudden wash of relief of all the pain and trouble I have carried within me. It is almost all gone. This is like a miracle and I know in my heart that this is my dog. The right decision was made. We’ve got this!”

Thank you Steve, it sure took you long enough to figure it out!

Chapter 14: Out to Lunch

"What's on the schedule for today?"

"I think we are going out to lunch to see how we all work with the dogs in a restaurant environment, Steve."

Good, it's time we get out of here and explore a bit. I need Steve to see all that I can do for him.

I follow Steve out to the car, we get in, and away we go. I actually like riding in the car and exploring the world. We always seem to go someplace new. Kimi was wonderful taking me places. Now Steve and I can do the same thing.

When we arrive at the restaurant, I take my place quietly under the table as instructed by Steve. I don't think anyone even knows I am here.

"I think I'll just have a bacon cheeseburger and a Coke." I hear Steve tell the waitress.

Even here on the ground, I can smell the food arriving. <sniff> <sniff> YEP that's bacon all right! I love it!! I'd love for Steve to share with me, but I know it is not allowed. So, I'll just wait here for him while he enjoys his lunch.

WOOPS! What's that? I turn and see that a piece of bacon has fallen from the table and has landed on my back. I just *know* everyone thinks I will whip around and snatch it. Instead, I simply do as I was trained and lay my head back down on the ground, at Steve's feet.

"Honey, did you see that! Gottie barely even reacted to the bacon falling on him. Is this dog even for real? Can he possibly be *this* good?"

I am happy that Steve is so proud of me.

We are a team; we will *always* be together, Steve and I.

Chapter 15: Squirrel!

It's Friday and they have set up a game we all call "SQUIRREL!" The team tries to distract us with toys and popcorn, throwing them at us or around the room while we work. Everyone thinks I will turn my head and check out the distraction, but my eyes are only on Steve. I don't want anything to happen that would cause them to take me away from him.

I know they all thought I would eat the bacon the other day, but I know the SQUIRREL game and I'm not going to let them beat me at it!

Chapter 16: My Valentine

Today is special, I can feel it through my entire body, I love that I now spend the nights in the room with Steve. We are all up early and Steve and the lady are busy getting ready. It feels as if I am not really even part of things today, for some reason.

They take me outside and one of the trainers takes me to the kennels. What? What's going on? Are they taking me away from Steve? NO, NO!! This is not acceptable! I want to stay with Steve, why doesn't everyone understand this by now.

I'm not in the kennel for too long when I get the most incredible surprise, Kimi is here! They let me out of the kennel and Kimi takes me to the big grassy area to play.

Kimi says to me, "It is a very special day for two reasons. First, it is Valentine's Day and you are still my special love. Two, you are going to fulfill your destiny by changing Steve's life. I know you have been waiting for this moment to prove yourself."

Kimi, sweet Kimi – I'm doing so well. Thank you for raising me and loving me. Have you met Steve? He is such a good man, but he is in so much pain. He needs me, Kimi. I love you, but Steve needs me more.

As we play together, I can see that they are setting up chairs and a stage. People keep coming in, much like the day Kimi brought me here and I began training. There is a lot of excitement, but I'm still concerned as to where Steve got off to and when he will be returning for me.

As crowds of people fill the chairs, I hear the voice of my Steve. Right now, he is just another person in the crowd, but at least I feel more at ease, knowing he is here.

There are many speeches and videos, and I see pictures of me as a puppy at Kimi's house. There are pictures of all the dogs, but I am clearly the most handsome. I think everyone sees that as well.

After one speech in particular, I hear them call Steve's name and then Mr. Gottlieb and Kimi's names. Afterward, they introduce me. Kimi takes my lead and we walk up to the ramp. Mr. Gottlieb joins us and we all walk up onto the stage. I see Steve at the other end. As we walk across to meet him, I feel the excitement growing inside of my heart. Yes, yes – I'm leaving with Steve!! Kimi hands my lead over to Steve as the crowd of people applaud. I'm glad EVERYONE is happy that Steve and I are together, because it *is* the best match possible.

The ceremony ends and people begin moving around. Kimi comes back over and gives Steve a gift. It is a CD of pictures of me at Kimi's house and all of the adventures we had together. Then Mr. Gottlieb walks over. Steve and Mr. Gottlieb talk for quite a while and I can see that they like each other. I am just so happy that everyone I love is here together today. I can't help but wonder what is next, though.

Chapter 17: A New Texas Cowboy

Hey! I remember this place! This is where that big metal tube took me from the place I was born and we came here. It still smells bad and the noise is terrible. I hope they don't put me in a crate again.

I stay close to Steve as we enter and walk through the building. There are people EVERYWHERE! I follow Steve and look for hazards that might upset him. After quite a long walk, we arrive at a place with chairs and a beautiful woman standing at a door. People walk up to her and hand her a piece of paper. They then disappear down a hallway.

I stand in line with Steve until we reach this woman. She smiles and nods at both of us and we walk through the door. The hallway is long and skinny and at the other end, there is still another door. <whew> I'm glad I don't have to help Steve open this one, it looks very thick and heavy.

We walk in and there are rows and rows of seats. We walk past a few of the seats and I see what looks like a wall. We turn and enter the row of seats along this wall they are calling the "bulkhead." I take my place at Steve's feet, where I belong. I curl up into a little ball and quickly go to sleep. It has been a busy few days and I am quite tired.

Everything finally settles down and I hear several announcements. I can feel Steve settling into his seat and then we start to move. It is very slow at first and then we pick up speed. Before I know it, we are moving extremely fast and I can guess what happens next. Yep, we are coming up off the ground again. We are flying!

This trip is much longer than my prior trip on an airplane, but thankfully, I am here with Steve, so it isn't as bad.

After a couple of hours, I hear the pretty lady announce that we will be landing at the Dallas/Fort Worth airport. I guess this is my new home. It really doesn't matter where I am, as long as I am with Steve.

The plane lands with a bump and we move slowly to a gate. Once the plane stops, everyone seems to stand up and move forward up the aisle. As they pass by our seats, they look down and see me. More than one person says, "Oh my! I didn't even know there was a dog on this plane!" I can feel Steve's heart swell with pride, and that makes me happy and proud as well.

Chapter 18: The Rose

"Gottie! We did it! It's the end of the day and the house looks perfect! We did laundry, folded everything, put it all away and NOTHING is still lying on the floor. Gottie, you are THE BEST! I love you, boy."

Of course, all I did today is follow Steve around and help him pick things up. Well, that and one other thing. Lately Steve sits and talks to me a lot, he tells me things from his past that are very sad, things that make him angry and depressed. I'm glad he tells me these things because I can better understand the burden he carries in his heart and in his soul. I just do my best to nuzzle up beside him and make certain he knows I am always here for him.

I knew we would make a really good pair. Every day Steve improves just a little. He seems happier, more relaxed and he moves around more and more.

The day is made especially wonderful when Steve's wife comes home from work. She comes in, looks around and realizes that she doesn't have to start her "second job;" she can just sit down and relax. Both of them are so much more at ease since I have been living here.

Today starts off and I just know something special will happen. Steve seems especially determined and upbeat. I can tell that Steve has an idea growing in his heart, he has a plan for the day unlike anything he has done before. I want to yell at him, "Go ahead, Steve, Just Do It! Together we can make it happen!"

Since I can't talk, I just go over and cuddle into him, making sure he knows he is safe and that he can move mountains if he just tries.

"Ok, Gottie, this is it. Are you ready?" Steve gets up, picks up my lead, hooks it on and off we go. We head out to the car and I quickly jump in. Steve and I have never gone out alone together, so this is a very special trip for both of us.

As we drive slowly down the street, Steve says, "Gottie, this is a big deal for me. I have not driven a car since the accident because there are far too many things that can upset and anger me. Being in public, around other people is also difficult. I know I can do this with you at my side."

Yes, Steve. I am here for you; *always*.

I wonder what Steve will buy at the store. When we arrive, it is not at all what I expect. We enter the market, Steve walks over to the flower counter, and he buys a rose wrapped in cellophane. He pays for it and we return to the car. I know it is important to him, but I thought we'd do more shopping together. Steve needs to take things slowly and I understand that. This trip is a far bigger step for him than it is for me. I just need to be patient and wait for him to catch up.

When we arrive home, Steve places the flower on the counter in the kitchen and returns to watch television with me. I can feel the pride and confidence coursing through his body. I don't fully understand why he is so happy, but his being happy makes me happy.

At the end of the day, the lady comes home and walks into the kitchen setting her things down. I hear her let out a little scream, turn to Steve and ask, "Did you go to the store by yourself today?"

Very firmly and proudly Steve says, "Yes, I did. Gottie and I went together."

Of course, I sat up a little straighter and looked at her with enough pride for both of us.

"I can't believe it! I just can't believe it!" she says, as she bursts into tears.

I can feel the tension and the burden ease off of her, just as it has been easing off of Steve. Because I am here, Steve is finding his independence and the lady realizes she doesn't have to worry about Steve all day long. I am here to help now! It is a happy day for all of us.

Chapter 19: I Meet the Parents

I'm enjoying my time with Steve, helping him, listening to him, and easing his pain. But I'm curious about his life beyond these walls. Where did he come from, who is his family, why is he always so sad?

Well, I've been here about a month and today it appears I am getting at least one of those questions answered. Steve is moving around the house, getting things together. I hear him say,

"I'm anxious for mom and dad to meet Gottie and see all he can do. I want them to know what an amazing dog my boy really is.

I follow Steve around the house wagging my tail! I know this means we are going for a ride and that is something that always brings me joy. I am also happy that Steve enjoys showing me off to people, just as I like showing Steve off to people as well.

We all head out to the car and start driving down the road. We arrive at this lovely home and I proudly exit the car and stand at attention waiting for Steve. As we walk up the front walkway, the door opens and this beautiful, radiant woman is standing there to greet us. She smiles broadly as Steve walks up to her. I did notice her also sneaking a peek at me and smiling a bit. That doesn't really surprise me though; people seem to take an instant liking to me!

Steve's mom gives him a hug, looks at me and then looks Steve in the face. She takes his face in her hands and says, "You are a completely changed man! Having this dog has changed you, it has taken the hurt, anger, and anxiety out of you. Steve, I could not be happier."

We had a nice afternoon together; both of Steve's parents are very nice and seem to like me. I know they are happy with Steve's progress and how my being with Steve has changed him.

Chapter 20: Oh, Now I Understand

Recently, Steve has been taking me to many events, mostly with puppies and their raisers. I keep looking to see if Kimi is there, but I know that is silly. Kimi is in California and I am a Texan now. Steve rarely says much, we just demonstrate some of the skills I use to help Steve. This is just to show the puppy raisers and others how much the puppies will learn before being matched with a client.

One special day, Steve takes a little more time getting dressed and we head off in the car. Steve tells me that we will be having lunch with Mr. Gottlieb, the man I am named after. He lives in Australia, but is staying at a hotel near the airport. He contacted Steve and asked if we would join him for lunch at his hotel.

I have not seen him since the graduation ceremony, but I look forward to thanking him again for letting me meet Steve.

When we enter the restaurant, Mr. Gottlieb proudly and confidently walks towards us. He introduces us to the staff at the hotel and tells everyone how he is the Dog-Father of this handsome dog, also named Gottlieb. I just beam from all of the attention; I am so proud.

Steve sits down at the table with Mr. Gottlieb, so I take my place underneath where I belong. While they talk, I remain at Steve's side to help him as needed.

Over lunch, I hear Mr. Gottlieb ask Steve to tell his story.

Mr. Gottlieb isn't the only one waiting to hear this. By the time Steve is finished, I think both of us are stunned. I learn that Steve has survived 13 explosions while serving time in Iraq, some in vehicles and some in open areas.

The events that affected Steve the most were losing eight of his ten men in explosions. The first story was the most gut wrenching and made me want to just curl up with Steve and rest my head on his chest, again. One of his men took his Humvee to a green or active fighting zone. It was part of a convoy that hit a daisy-chain of IED explosives on the road. This is where one explosive trips the others in succession.

They called down to his base and Steve learned that his man had had both his arms and legs blown off. They were making a plea for anyone with type AB blood to come up and donate. He immediately stood and announced that he was heading up there. He was ordered not to go for two reasons, one because he was about to go on leave and two because he was not the same blood type. He said, "I am blood type O, I am a universal donor. Just let me go up there, maybe I can help in some way." "Soldier you are about to go on leave, just stay here," was the response. Steve, not to be denied, replied, "Then cancel my leave, just let me help my man!"

Some time passed and Steve was finally told that it was too late, that his man had died. "If I had gone, maybe this man would not be dead."

With this event in his heart, Steve returned home on leave and was pretty much a zombie the entire time. He said he mostly just sat on the front porch drinking and smoking and thinking about what had happened in Iraq.

As Steve tells these stories, he periodically reaches down and scratches me on the head. I raise my head to let him know I am here for him.

Then he tells us about another event where five more of his men were killed in an explosion of a dump truck loaded with mortar shells. It was an ambush at a traffic control point.

Clearly, the most difficult story for Steve to tell was when he lost one of his last men in December 2005. The soldier was driving a Bradley Fighting Vehicle, which is similar to a small tank. The vehicle drove over an IED and the explosion knocked the driver unconscious. The vehicle kept rolling to the street. Steve heard the call "Contact IED" and his heart fell into his stomach. He was told that they could not get the driver out of the vehicle because it was on fire. Steve knew the driver as he was one of his men. Steve was not about to do nothing and lose yet another man. He drove as fast as possible to the site of the explosion. When he arrived, everyone was just standing around, watching the vehicle burn. He asked, "Is the driver still in there? Why didn't you get him out?" In spite of the explosives on the vehicle and that it was on fire, Steve ran to the vehicle and climbed onto it as it was burning. When he kicked open the hatch, smoke of noxious gas rose from inside. Steve reached in and saw the driver slumped over in his seat. As Steve grabbed him to pull him out, burning his arms, he realized that the man was dead. Steve was so angry that he grabbed the man's vest and pulled him out anyway. He rolled off the Bradley with the body. After Steve laid the body down on the ground, the medic confirmed that nothing could be done.

Even from my place lying on the floor, I can feel Steve's heart heavy with sadness. I stand and nuzzle his hand with my nose, gently licking his palm. I now understand the anguish my Steve carries and now my heart is heavy as well. My poor Steve, my warrior.

Steve tells of the accident in California and his struggles in finding a service dog. He finishes by telling Mr. Gottlieb that Canine Companions pretty much saved his life.

I'm so glad I finally understand Steve's hurt and anguish. I know why he is in so much pain. Gladly, though, I can also feel that pain easing with me at his side.

"Steve, would you be willing to tell your story to the board of directors of Canine Companions? I think it is important they hear first-hand how our program changes lives," I hear Mr. Gottlieb ask Steve.

"Mel, I want to help but that is a pretty big request. I'm not comfortable speaking in front of a group of people and I've never really told my story to more than one person at a time." There is a pause as he ponders this a moment and then Steve continues, "You know what? I will do whatever you need. This organization has been so good to me starting from my very first phone call to the regional facility in Oceanside. I need to give back to Canine Companions so just tell me what is next. Maybe the best way for me to deal with my PTSD is immersion therapy, throwing myself out there in a sink or swim situation. Yes, Mel, I'll do whatever I can."

I look up at Steve with great pride in my heart. He is such a fine man.

Steve and I head home and I can sense that something big is about to happen for both of us.

Chapter 21: Ambassadors

Here we are in front of the entire board of directors of Canine Companions. I am at Steve's side and I can tell he is quite nervous. He tells his story in the same manner he told Mr. Gottlieb in the restaurant. As before, he periodically reaches down to touch me for reassurance.

At the end of Steve's speech, there is not a dry eye on the board. Someone says, "We need to get these two out there and speaking. How can we create a program for some of our graduates to speak at various events?"

I know at that moment that Steve and I will be talking in front of a lot more people in the near future.

This eventually leads to Canine Companions forming a small group of ambassadors for the organization, initially it is just four of us. We receive requests to fly all over the country and speak at various gatherings. I am always so proud of Steve, how he just pushes through his fears, gets up, and speaks. Of course, I am always at his side providing whatever support I can.

“Gottie, we are going to see your best friend Mel today. We are picking him up at the airport and having dinner with a district court judge, Judge Ed Kinkeade. Mel wants me to tell my story to him as well.”

I don’t have to do too much to get ready to go out, but Steve does his best to look sharp.

We drive to the airport and pick up Mel and then head to a barbeque restaurant in Dallas. Apparently, it is the judge’s favorite place. Oh my, the smells are almost more than I can handle. It is all I can do not to misbehave and make Steve look bad. I do control myself and act as a gentleman.

We meet this very distinguished looking gentleman and his beautiful wife. They are both very nice to me and to Steve.

Steve tells his story to Judge Kinkeade and when he finishes, the judge looks at him and says, “Steve, we are trying to get a new Canine Companions regional facility built here in the Dallas/Fort Worth area. Will you please join me and another graduate, also a veteran, to speak to the board of Baylor, Scott, & White Health? The board needs to fully understand why this facility is not simply a convenience for those seeking service dogs, it is a necessity. Currently, people in Texas and other areas in the south must travel to either California or Florida for Team Training. This region is not currently well served by us, but the demand for our dogs continues growing."

I don't think anyone noticed, but I wagged my tail briefly. My Steve is becoming a very important man. I know this is helping build back his confidence as well. It isn't just me, his entire world is changing.

Because of these meetings, construction begins on the new South Central Region training center in Irving, Texas, just east of Fort Worth. It is located on the campus of Baylor, Scott, & White Health and is the only regional facility associated with a health care company. On its opening, it will serve only Texas.

Steve regularly receives invitations to speak and he and I fly all over the country to meet people and talk about Canine Companions. Usually, the director of the South Central Region campus joins us.

On one of our trips, we fly to Washington, D.C. to meet with then Senator Al Franken to discuss laws governing service dogs. Our concerns are in regards to people buying vests for their untrained dogs and passing them off as if they are of the same high caliber as me and my fellow canine colleagues from Canine Companions. Misbehaving dogs give all of us a bad name and make it more difficult for people to accept us into their businesses and homes.

One of the most exciting meetings is with President George W. Bush at the Wounded Warrior Open golf tournament. Steve talks with him for quite some time and Mr. Bush did something you almost never see. He takes Steve's head in the crook of his arm and gives him a nuggie. It seems a little odd, but Steve is very impressed and pleased to receive so high a Presidential honor. If Steve is happy, I am happy.

One fun adventure we have that firmly establishes me as a Cowboy is when the organization Defenders of Freedom is invited to tour the new Cowboy Stadium in Arlington, Texas before it is open to the public or used for any game. We are on the field when Steve throws me a long pass with one of the toy footballs passed out to everyone. I'm in the end zone when I catch the pass. So, technically, I catch the very first touchdown pass in Cowboy stadium.

I have one other dubious Cowboy Stadium honor. After we play on the field a while, I can sense nature calling to me. I walk over to Steve and let him know my plight. He talks to one of the staff members and asks where he might easily exit the stadium and tells him why. The staff member points to the edge of the Astro turf and explains that there are drains along the sideline to handle the rain when it falls through the open stadium roof. He tells Steve to simply take me over there. So, Gottlieb, wonder dog, not only catches the first touchdown pass, I am also the first to pee on the field, forever marking that territory as my own.

What adventures Steve and I have together!

Chapter 22: The Winds of Change

Something has changed, but I'm not totally sure what has happened. Steve is just not himself these days. In spite of all the wonderful things we do together and all he has accomplished, he seems depressed again. I try my best to pep him up, but am not successful.

The tension at home is thick between Steve and the lady. Things do not seem to be going well. Eventually, their marriage ends and Steve and I are alone. Although this creates problems for Steve, it eventually creates new opportunities for me to further show him just how much I can help.

With the lady out of the picture, Steve must now assume many of the household duties she performed. Many of these duties are difficult for Steve and he works with me to teach me new commands and behaviors. He puts straps on the laundry baskets and I learn to pull the laundry from the bedroom into the laundry room. This is just one of the many new tasks I perform for him. I don't mind, I'm just happy to help in any way possible. Steve's mom also comes over and helps out, but I think I help the most.

Because of this, I feel that Steve and I grow even closer, something I didn't even think was possible.

With all of the changes at home, we limit our traveling and our work as ambassadors. I miss meeting new people on our travels, but my top priority is helping Steve live his life day to day. The glamor side of my job was apparently just a temporary perk.

Because of something they call Covid, we spend even more time at home. Steve becomes more comfortable and independent and our lives resume a more normal cadence.

There is another change happening; I am starting to slow down. I have more difficulties jumping in and out of the car, so much so that Steve sometimes has to help me by picking me up. I feel embarrassed that I have trouble doing such simple tasks. I even have trouble jumping up onto the bed. I don't like to admit it, but as indestructible as I like to believe I am, I am getting older. I still think like a puppy, but my body is starting to give out here and there.

In spite of this, all I need to hear is the sound of Steve picking up his car keys or the door to the washer or dryer being opened and I still jump up and am ready to work. When I hear him crinkle a piece of paper or wrapper when he is on the couch, I'll still run over to take it from him to throw it in the trash. I'm still me, I'm still Gottie the wonder dog! Nothing will ever change that.

Chapter 23: Retirement

I am about eleven years old when one day Steve calls me over to him. He looks deeply into my eyes and removes my working vest. He pauses briefly, and then removes my collar and sets both of them aside. He takes my face in his two hands, he smiles at me, and then kisses me on my head. "My good and faithful servant," he says, "I think it is time for you to retire. You have been slowing down and I can tell that many of the tasks you attempt are painful to you. You saved my life, boy, you made me see that my life can go on. You were there when I needed you most. You mean everything to me, Gottie, but I love you too much to make you suffer.

"The veterinarian has checked you over and you have the early signs of arthritis. I've talked to the people At Canine Companions and they agree that you have earned your right to just relax and take it easy."

But, Steve.... I'm not ready. I'm here to help you forever. I love working for you and helping you in life. You are my entire life. You are my Steve. I feel I am letting Steve down, but Steve is correct, my body and my will are no longer on the same page. Steve does things to make my life easier. One thing I love is that he takes the crate I first used when I came home with him and converts it into a type of staircase I use to climb up onto his bed. I am so thankful that I can still cuddle up next to him and let him know I am his main man.

One day I hear Steve's mom ask, "Have you thought about applying for another dog?"

"No, not yet. I just can't do that to Gottie. I don't want him to think for a moment he is being replaced because he isn't good enough. He has gone above and beyond any expectation I had for him. I cannot hurt him, his pride, his ego and his love for me by bringing in a 'replacement.' No, I'll do without for as long as possible. Gottie cannot be replaced even though having him has changed my life."

I look up at Steve and try to say, "In spite of my getting older, I am still the best at what I do, and I will do everything to prove that until the day I am gone."

"Gottie, you have gone so far beyond anything I could have expected. You have done more than I could ever ask and you have done it all with a smile on your face and that wonderful prideful spring in your step. I know you are proud of your work and I want you to know that I think you are the absolute best dog Canine Companions has ever placed with anyone."

Thank you, Steve. I love you more than my heart can even contain. God has given me the best life possible because He brought me to you.

Epilogue

From Steve:

With Gottlieb, I was able to do things that were beyond my abilities after the accident. These limitations made me feel less than human. Simply bending over and picking something up was sometimes more than I could handle. With Gottie, all things became possible and I became my old self again. My confidence soared.

What Gottie really turned out to be for me was another battle buddy, in fact, he became one of those men who I lost in the war. In some ways, he became a surrogate for all of them. He was able to watch out for me as much as I watched out for him. He could keep a distance between strangers and me when I needed it. From his looking around and perking up his ears, I could look in the same direction to see whatever might create a problem for me.

We became so attuned to each other that he was like a second pair of eyes and ears. Because of this, I could relax a little because I did not always need to be so hyper-vigilant, a problem often associated with PTSD.

Not only can I now do what once seemed impossible, Gottie also helped me by opening doors when my hands were full as well as turning off lights when I was already in bed. These are just some of the special things he did for me.

From the author:

As remarkable as this story is, it is only one of many from Canine Companions. When I speak to groups, doing fundraising, I tell the true story of a little girl who had used a wheelchair for mobility since birth. At about eight years old, her mother contacted Canine Companions and she received her service dog. Months later she was interviewed and asked how the dog had changed her life. Like Steve, the dog helped her by picking items up off the floor, turning on and off lights and helping with opening and closing doors. But these things were not what she mentioned to the interviewer. She said, "I exist now." The interviewer, surprised by her answer asked, "What do you mean?" she replied, "You have to understand that as a child in a power chair, no one looks, smiles, or talks to you. Now, because of this dog, people look at my dog and then smile at me. They come over and ask me about my dog. I'm now part of the world that everyone else takes for granted. In school, I was the odd girl everyone avoided, now I am the girl with the cool dog."

These dogs effect change in people's lives in ways we can barely fathom. I challenge every reader of this book who has never done so, to find the closest Canine Companions regional center and attend a graduation. It is one of the most moving experiences you will ever have and I think it will change your life, just as it has changed mine.

God Bless.

Playing in Kimi's Back Yard

The Label on Gottlieb's Crate at Canine Companions

Holding the touchdown pass at Cowboy Stadium

"Steve, I'm ready"

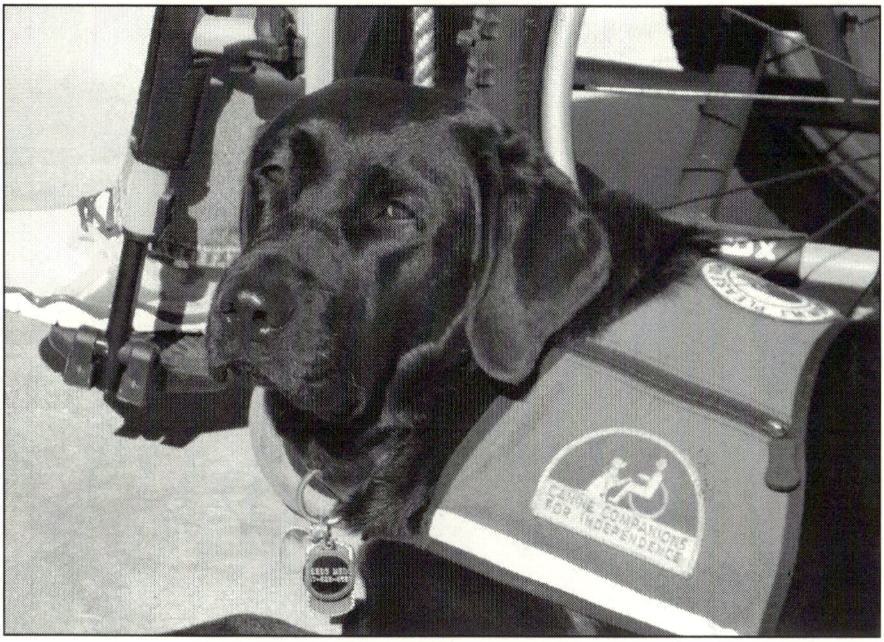

Working with Steve in his wheelchair

Helping Steve pick up simple objects

Helping Steve pick up simple objects

Steve speaking about Canine Companions

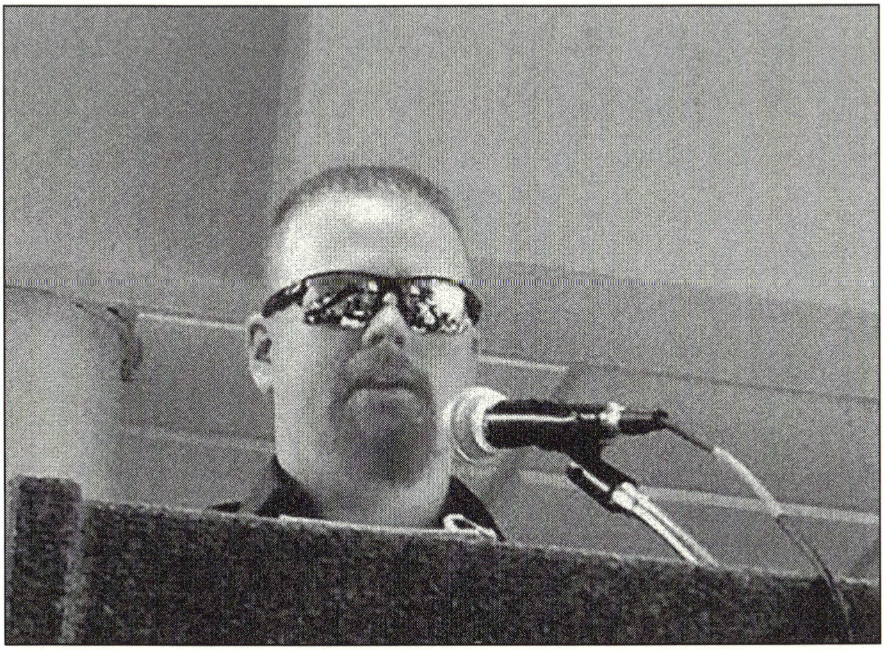

At the NASA Space Center in Florida

Meeting President George W. Bush

You've Got a Friend in Me!

The Author Interviewing Gottlieb

About Canine Companions

Canine Companions is a national non-profit organization that enhances the lives of people with disabilities by providing expertly trained service dogs and ongoing support free of charge. Canine Companions is leading the service dog industry so our clients and their dogs can live with greater independence. We provide service dogs to adults, children and veterans with disabilities and facility dogs to professionals working in healthcare, criminal justice and educational settings. Since our founding in 1975, our dogs and all follow-up services are provided at no cost to our clients.

Independence shouldn't be limited to those who look or live a certain way. Disability reaches all races, classes and backgrounds, and Canine Companions will too. Clients come to Canine Companions because of our reputation, the quality of our dogs, the experience of our training staff and the desire to lead life with greater independence. We are committed to providing services to all qualified clients.

Learn more at canine.org.

OTHER BOOKS BY THOMAS MARTIN, AVAILABLE ON AMAZON AND ON TMARTINBOOKS.COM

From Rage to Redemption: The Tragic & Inspirational Life of J. David Norcott, Jr.

One Percent: My Journey Overcoming Heart Disease

Just Do This One Thing: A Guide to Chronic Good Health

More Bang for Your Bucks: An Insider's Guide to Basic Financial Decisions

Ten Steps to Reversing Autism: A Natural, Organic, Dietary Approach

No More Heart Attacks: A 10 Step Protocol to Reversing Heart Disease

So, Why Did You Become a Mason: Travelers Taking Their First Steps Seeking Light